The Magic School Bus
Inside a Beehive

The Magic School Bus
Inside a Beehive

By Joanna Cole   **Illustrated by Bruce Degen**

SCHOLASTIC PRESS / *New York*

The author and illustrator wish to thank
Professor Mark L. Winston, Department of Biological Sciences, Simon Fraser University,
British Columbia, Canada, for his assistance in preparing this book.

For their helpful advice and consultation, thanks also to Ray Pupedis,
Division of Entomology, Yale-Peabody Museum of Natural History, New Haven, Connecticut;
Eric H. Erickson, Center Director, Carl Hayden Bee Research Center, Tucson, Arizona;
and Mark Richardson, who kindly gave us a tour of his beehive.

Library of Congress Cataloging-in-Publication Data

Cole, Joanna.
The magic school bus inside a beehive / by Joanna Cole ; illustrated by Bruce Degen.
p.   cm.
Summary: Ms. Frizzle takes her class on a field trip to a beehive in her magic school bus.
ISBN 0-590-44684-3
1. Honey bee—Juvenile literature. 2. Beehives—Juvenile literature.
[1. Honey bee. 2. Bees. 3. Beehives. 4. Honey.] I. Degen, Bruce, ill. II. Title.
QL568.A6C565   1996
585.79′9—dc20   95-38288
CIP
AC

12 11 10 9 8 7 6 5 4 3 2 1   6 7 8 9/9 0 1/0

Printed in the U.S.A.   36

First printing, September 1996

The display type was set in Cooper Black Shaded Italic.
The text type was set in Bookman Light 14 pt. on 18 lead.

The illustrator used pen and ink, watercolor, color pencil, and gouache for the paintings in this book.

To my
honey, Phil.

J.C.

To
Will Tressler
and Jim Setz, and
all the busy bees who
are building our new hive.

B.D.

"What a perfect spring day!"
said Ms. Frizzle, looking out the window.
We thought it was perfect, too —
perfect for playing softball.
But the Friz had something else in mind.
"It's just right for observing honey bees!"

BEE OBSERVANT
LOOK CLOSELY AT INSECTS

INSECT CHECKLIST
ALL ADULT INSECTS:
ALWAYS HAVE 6 LEGS
ALWAYS HAVE 3 BODY SECTIONS
ABDOMEN
THORAX
HEAD
USUALLY HAVE WINGS
USUALLY HAVE ANTENNAE
Fly

Honey bees are insects. Here are some other insects.

THERE ARE MORE INSECT SPECIES ON EARTH THAN ALL OTHER ANIMALS PUT TOGETHER!

YES, BUT DO THEY ALL HAVE TO BE IN OUR CLASSROOM?

IS A SPIDER AN INSECT?

No! SPIDERS HAVE EIGHT LEGS AND TWO BODY SECTIONS.

SPIDERS ARE RELATIVES OF INSECTS

DOROTHY ANN'S BIG BOOK OF BEES

LUNCH

Wasp

Cockroach

Ant

Housefly

We had been studying about all different kinds of insects.
Now Ms. Frizzle said she had found a beekeeper who would show us his honey bee hives.

"The beekeeper is visiting his hives today. We'll meet him there," said the Friz, and she swept out the door.

As we boarded the old school bus,
Ms. Frizzle talked and talked
about honey bees.
"They make a delicious food
for us to eat," she said.
"They help many plants survive.
And they are wonderful examples
of social insects!"

BEES ARE MY FAVORITE INSECTS.

WHAT IS YOUR FAVORITE INSECT, ARNOLD?

...I'M NOT THE KIND OF PERSON WHO HAS A FAVORITE INSECT.

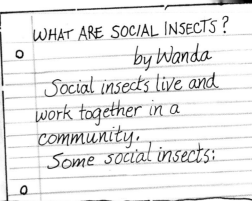

Ants nest in the ground.

Paper wasps make a nest out of wood pulp.

Bumble bees nest in grass-lined holes in the ground.

Termites nest in wood.

A WORD FROM DOROTHY ANN
Social comes from a
word that means
"friend" or "partner."

WHY DO BEES STING?
by Phoebe

Stinging is the way bees protect their hive. Bees usually sting only if they have to. That's because they die soon after they sting.

I'LL STING, BUT ONLY FOR A GOOD CAUSE...

...SUCH AS SAVING THE HIVE.

Honey bees have barbs, or hooks, on the end of their stingers.

STINGER   BARB

When a honey bee stings, her stinger gets stuck in the victim's skin. The stinger is pulled out of the bee's body, and the bee **dies**.

10

Ms. Frizzle drove out into the country and parked the bus next to the hives. The beekeeper was late, so Frizzie took out a picnic basket. "Some light refreshments will pass the time while we wait," she said. Sometimes, our teacher has *good* ideas!

BEES USUALLY WILL NOT STING, UNLESS YOU TOUCH THEM, ANNOY THEM, OR GET TOO CLOSE TO THEIR HIVE.

MAY WE CLOSE THE WINDOWS, PLEASE?

HONEY

But just as she opened a jar of honey, her elbow knocked a strange little lever. The honey jar fell, and we heard a weird buzzing sound.

It was the bus. It was vibrating, and getting smaller. So was everything in it — including *us!*

ALLERGIC TO BEE STINGS
by Ralphie
Some people get very sick and can even die from bee stings.
They have to carry special medicine.

11

Before we knew it, the bus looked like a little beehive, and we looked like real bees!
We really did!
"All out, class," buzzed the Friz.

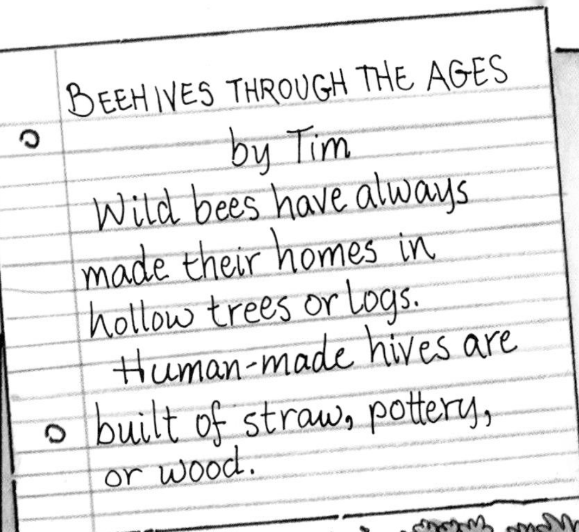

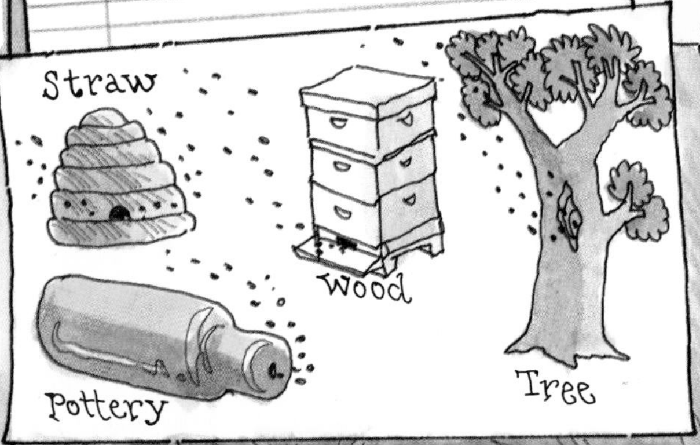

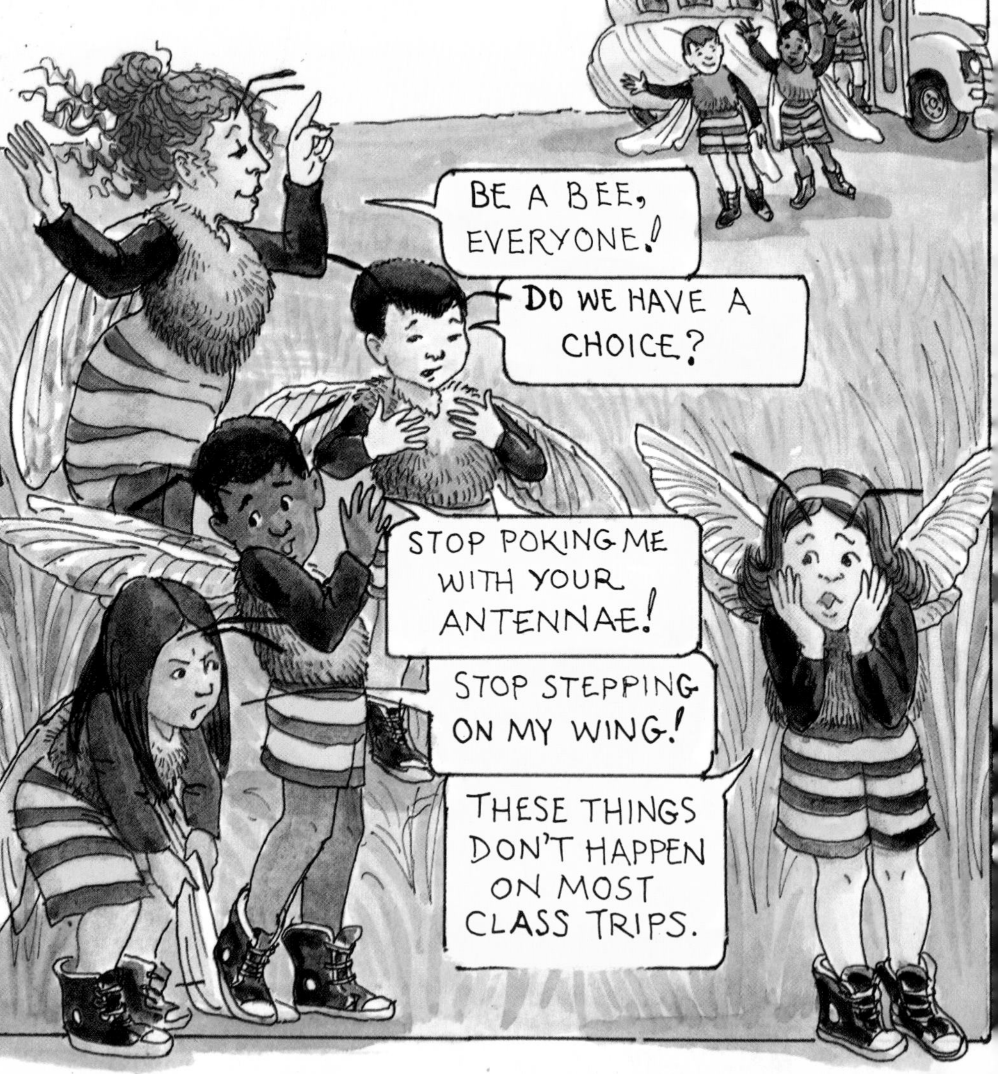

BE A BEE, EVERYONE!

DO WE HAVE A CHOICE?

STOP POKING ME WITH YOUR ANTENNAE!

STOP STEPPING ON MY WING!

THESE THINGS DON'T HAPPEN ON MOST CLASS TRIPS.

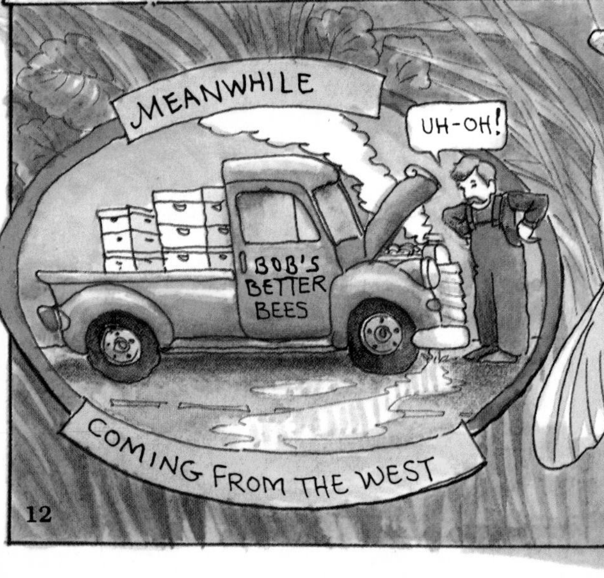

MEANWHILE

UH-OH!

BOB'S BETTER BEES

COMING FROM THE WEST

One by one, we stepped out the door and looked over at the nearest hive. At the entrance, worker bees were standing guard.

"Guard bees usually keep out bees from other hives," said the Friz.

ENTRANCE

GUARD BEE IN POSITION TO MEET INCOMING BEES

ACCORDING TO MY RESEARCH, GUARD BEES WILL BITE AND STING STRANGE BEES.

DO WE QUALIFY AS "STRANGE BEES"?

NO DOUBT ABOUT IT!

DOROTHY ANN'S BIG BOOK OF BEES

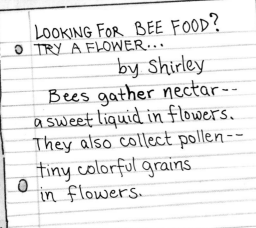

LOOKING FOR BEE FOOD?
TRY A FLOWER...
by Shirley
Bees gather nectar --
a sweet liquid in flowers.
They also collect pollen --
tiny colorful grains
in flowers.

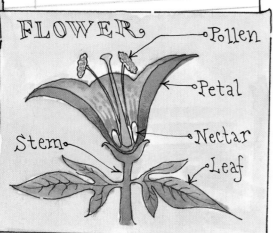

FLOWER

Pollen

Petal

Stem

Nectar

Leaf

"There is *one* time when guard bees may let in a strange bee," said Ms. Frizzle. "Sometimes a hive may 'adopt' a lost bee — *if* it is carrying a lot of bee food. All bee food comes from flowers.

BEES EAT ONLY NECTAR AND POLLEN, AND FOODS THEY MAKE FROM NECTAR AND POLLEN.

WHAT? NO CHIPS?

THE AVERAGE BEE VISITS THOUSANDS OF FLOWERS EVERY DAY.

NOW I KNOW WHY THEY CALL THEM BUSY BEES!

"We'll have to visit flowers and get bee food in order to gain entrance to the hive. Follow that bee!" shouted the Friz. We flew after a bee that was headed toward some bright flowers.

MEANWHILE

COMING FROM THE EAST

EXACTLY WHAT DOES SHE MEAN BY "GAIN ENTRANCE TO THE HIVE"?

SHE MEANS GO INSIDE IT.

I WAS AFRAID OF THAT...

FLYING IS FUN!

BUZZ OFF!

15

BEES HELP FLOWERS MAKE SEEDS
by Alex
As bees visit flowers, they pollinate them. This means they carry pollen from one flower to another.

Pollen
Pollen tube
Fertilized egg
Ovary
Honey stomach (inside body)
Tongue
Nectar

When a grain of pollen joins with an egg cell in a flower, a seed begins to grow.

MANY PLANTS CANNOT MAKE SEEDS UNLESS BEES POLLINATE THEIR FLOWERS.

WE NEED BEES!

"Observe our bee, children, and do exactly what she does!" Ms. Frizzle called. The bee stuck her long tubelike tongue deep into a flower and pumped out nectar. We each did the same with a rubber tube. "The bee carries the nectar in a pouch called the honey stomach," Frizzie told us. We carried our nectar in a tiny bottle.

BEE POLLINATE THEM! KIND TO FLOWERS

BE A BEE! COLLECT NECTAR AND POLLEN.

Pollen grains rubbed off the flower
and stuck onto the bee's "fur."
With her front and middle legs,
she combed off the pollen and packed it
into pollen baskets —
pouches on her back legs.
Then she returned to the hive.
We packed our pollen and went along.

BEES HELP MAKE FOOD FOR PEOPLE
by John
Bees pollinate many crop plants -- plants that give us our food.

Apple

Blueberry

Squash

Orange

AT MY OLD SCHOOL, WE NEVER COLLECTED FLOWER PRODUCTS.

IF WE HAVE A LOT, MAYBE THE BEES WON'T STING US.

I'M GETTING EXTRA!

POLLEN BASKET

POLLEN BASKET

WE NEED BEES!

BEES "TALK" WITH SMELLS!
by Amanda Jane

<u>PHEROMONES</u> are body chemicals that allow animals to "talk" to each other by smell.

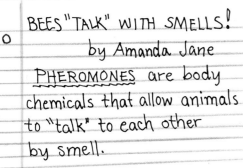

WHEW! DO YOU HAVE TO "TALK" SO LOUD?

With pheromones, bees send each other many messages. Here are some of them:
"I'm a hive-mate."
"I'm a stranger."
"I'm a worker."
"I'm the queen bee!"
"Danger! Danger!"
"Defend the hive!"

Bees don't talk in words, but they <u>do</u> communicate.

One by one, we landed at the hive.
The Friz sprayed us with a bee pheromone —
a chemical that bees make.
Now we smelled like bees.
Then came the scary part.

THERE MAY BE AS MANY AS 60,000 BEES IN ONE HIVE, CLASS.

WHAT IF THEY NOTICE WE'RE NOT REAL BEES?

SPRAY ME AGAIN PLEASE, MS. FRIZZLE!

BE A BEE

BEE BRAVE KIDS!

We held our breath as the guard bees brushed us with their antennae, smelling us. If they fell for our trick, we'd get into the hive. If they didn't, we'd get into big trouble!

WE'RE TAKING A BIG CHANCE.

I'LL BUZZ TO THAT!

WORK ORDERS
- ☑ Guard entrance
- ☑ Clean hive
- ☑ Build comb
- ☑ Make honey
- ☑ Fan wings to cool hive
- ☑ Tend queen
- ☑ Feed baby bees
- ☑ Collect pollen and nectar

WHO'S WHO IN THE HIVE?
by Michael

In a honey bee colony, there are three castes, or kinds, of bees:

1. The QUEEN: Her job is to lay eggs, eggs, and more eggs!

QUEEN

2. The WORKERS: They are all female bees that usually do not lay eggs. Workers do almost all the jobs in the hive.

3. The DRONES are all male bees. A male bee's only job is to mate with a queen.

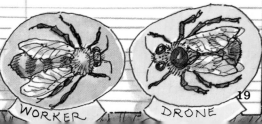

WORKER   DRONE

A BEEHIVE COMES IN SECTIONS
by Molly

TOP
INSIDE COVER
"SUPER" FRAMES (HOLD THE EXTRA HONEY WE TAKE TO EAT)
QUEEN EXCLUDER (KEEPS QUEEN IN LOWER SECTIONS)
FRAME WITH COMB
CELLS (HOLD BABY BEES, HONEY, AND POLLEN)
DEEP HIVE BOX
ENTRANCE
LANDING PLATFORM

WE ARE HERE

MEANWHILE

WATER

BOB'S BETTER BEES

COMING FROM THE WEST

The guards smelled our bee spray
and our bee food. They let us pass!
Other workers took our nectar
and bustled off with it.
"Hooray! We're free to explore the hive!"
sang out Ms. Frizzle.

The first thing we saw was our bee.
She was doing a strange dance.
Other bees crowded around her,
touching her and listening to her.
Ms. Frizzle said the dance was a "language."
With her dance, the bee "told" others
which way to go to the flowers
she had found.

OUR BEE

MEANWHILE

SNIFF
SNIFF

COMING FROM THE EAST

21

THE ROUND DANCE
by Phil

This dance tells bees that a food source is close to the hive. The dancing bee walks in a circle, then turns around and goes the other way.

The other bees go outside and fly in a circular pattern near the hive until they find the flowers.

BEE-HIVE

The dance helped the bees find food faster. They did not have to waste time looking for it. They flew off in the direction of the flowers we had visited.

BEES HAVE MANY DANCES.

DOROTHY ANN'S BIG BOOK OF BEES

EACH DANCE "SAYS" SOMETHING DIFFERENT.

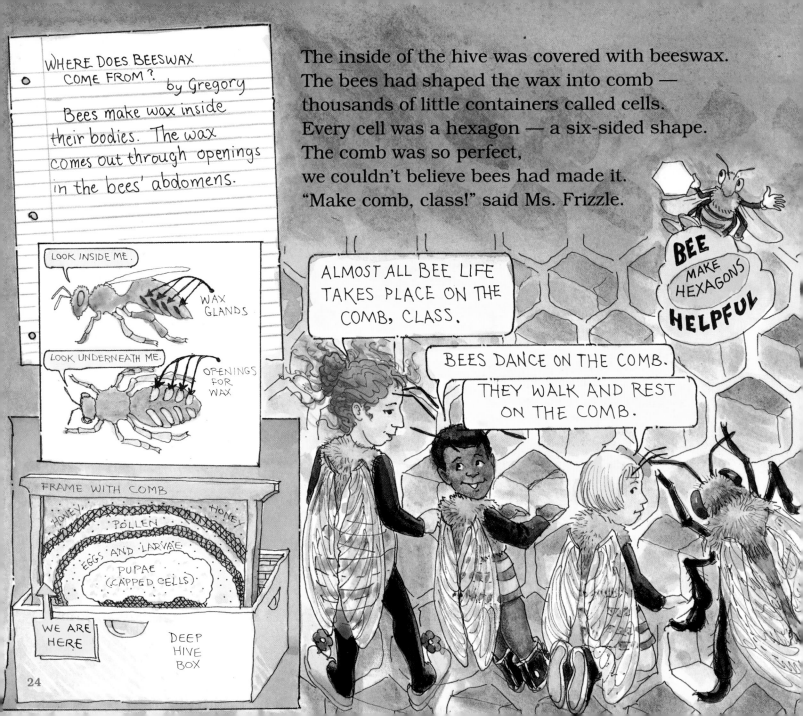

WHERE DOES BEESWAX COME FROM?
by Gregory

Bees make wax inside their bodies. The wax comes out through openings in the bees' abdomens.

LOOK INSIDE ME.

WAX GLANDS

LOOK UNDERNEATH ME.

OPENINGS FOR WAX

FRAME WITH COMB

HONEY   HONEY

POLLEN

EGGS AND LARVAE

PUPAE (CAPPED CELLS)

WE ARE HERE

DEEP HIVE BOX

The inside of the hive was covered with beeswax.
The bees had shaped the wax into comb —
thousands of little containers called cells.
Every cell was a hexagon — a six-sided shape.
The comb was so perfect,
we couldn't believe bees had made it.
"Make comb, class!" said Ms. Frizzle.

ALMOST ALL BEE LIFE TAKES PLACE ON THE COMB, CLASS.

BEES DANCE ON THE COMB.
THEY WALK AND REST ON THE COMB.

BEE MAKE HEXAGONS HELPFUL

We did our best, but our cells
came out pretty lopsided.
Luckily, the bees didn't notice us.
They just tore down our cells
and built them over again.
Other bees were busy with other jobs,
such as making honey.

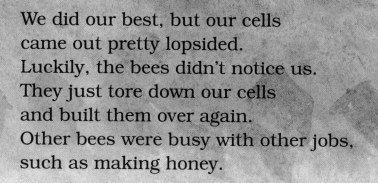

BEES RAISE BABIES IN THE COMB CELLS.

THEY STORE NECTAR AND POLLEN IN THE CELLS.

THEY MAKE HONEY IN THE CELLS, TOO.

THAT'S SWEET OF THEM.

HOW BEES MAKE COMB
by Rachel

A bee uses her back and middle legs to pass wax to her front legs.
Then she chews and shapes the wax into cells.

Honey bees make the comb cells tilt up so the honey doesn't drip out!

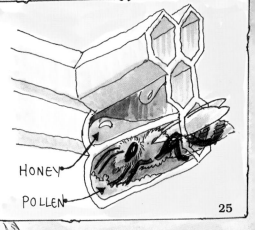

HONEY

POLLEN

25

MEANWHILE COMING FROM THE WEST

We saw the bees changing nectar into honey.
First, they added chemicals
from glands inside their heads.
The chemicals changed the
nectar-sugars into honey-sugars.
Then they spread droplets out
and fanned them with their wings.
This dried up most of the water —
leaving the honey thick, sticky,
and extra-sweet.
We fanned, too, and helped make honey.

26

Ms. Frizzle said it was okay to eat some honey, as long as we left plenty for the bees.
"They need a good supply of honey to help them survive over the winter," she explained.

IT'S COZY IN A BEEHIVE.

IT'S TASTY IN A BEEHIVE.

IT'S EASY TO HELP WITH THIS JOB!

HONEY IS GOOD FOOD!
by Molly
Honey is a very good food for bees, humans, and other animals. But human babies under one year should not eat raw honey.

YOU'RE NOT OLD ENOUGH FOR HONEY, HONEY.

HONEY

BEE EAT HONEY! HAPPY

We stopped eating honey long enough
to notice a bunch of worker bees nearby.
They were tending a larger bee
with a long thin body.
She was the queen bee!
As the queen walked from cell to cell,
she laid a small white egg in each one.

The workers touched the queen with their antennae,
they licked her with their tongues,
and they fed her by mouth-to-mouth exchange.

HOW TO FEED BABY BEES
by Amanda Jane

Nurse bees make baby food in glands inside their heads. This is called "brood food." The nurses squeeze out the food right into the larvae's cells.

SOMETIMES LARVAE ARE <u>SWIMMING</u> IN FOOD.

SOUNDS DELICIOUS.

Older larvae also eat honey and "bee bread," a food that is a mix of pollen and honey.

In some cells, we saw wormlike creatures. "These are larvae — baby bees that hatched out of the eggs," said Ms. Frizzle. Nurse bees were feeding the babies.

THESE WORMLIKE THINGS ARE BABY BEES?

THEY DON'T LOOK LIKE BEES AT ALL.

THEY WILL, KEESHA, THEY WILL. ALL THEY NEED IS THREE THINGS: FOOD, WARMTH, AND TIME.

The larvae did nothing but eat fast and grow fast.
Every time they got too big for their skins,
they molted, or shed their skins.
Then they started eating and growing again!

BE A BEE! FEED THE LARVAE!

LARVAE ARE LUCKY.

THEY GET ROOM SERVICE.

THE ROYAL TREATMENT
by Phil

If a hive becomes too crowded, workers get ready to start a new hive.
First they build some special upside-down cells for new queen bees.

Queen Larva

Nurse bees feed ordinary female larvae special food called "royal jelly." Then the larvae develop into queens.

IF A FEMALE LARVA GETS ROYAL JELLY, SHE BECOMES A QUEEN.

IF NOT, SHE ENDS UP AS A WORKER.

ROYAL JELLY

"When it is big enough, the larva stops eating," said the Friz. "It spins a silk cocoon around itself. Now it is called a pupa.
The nurse bees put a wax top on the cell.
Inside, the pupa doesn't eat or grow bigger.
It changes into an adult bee.
This is called metamorphosis.

32

"When the pupae have finished
changing into adult bees,
they chew their way out of their cells,"
continued Ms. Frizzle.
We saw new worker bees emerging.
They let the air dry them off
and started working right away.
Meanwhile, we heard excited buzzing.
What was happening?

BEE GROW UP! ADULT

NOW THE METAMORPHOSIS IS COMPLETE, CHILDREN.

THE BEES ARE ALL GROWN UP.

I'M SO PROUD OF THEM.

THE ROAD FROM **EGG** TO **BEE**

EGG LARVA PUPA ADULT

SWARMING BEES USUALLY DON'T STING
by Phoebe
Usually bees sting because they have a hive to protect. A swarm does not. It's a colony of bees that's "between hives."

WE'RE LOOKING FOR AN EMPTY BEEHIVE...

...OR A NICE HOLLOW TREE.

SWARM

MEANWHILE

THE BEAR FINDS THE HIVE

The queen was leaving the hive! And she was taking almost half the workers with her! They flew away in a thick swarm. What would become of the hive now?

EXIT

SWARMING IS NATURE'S WAY OF STARTING NEW BEEHIVES.

BUT HOW CAN THE OLD HIVE SURVIVE WITHOUT THE QUEEN?

THERE'S NO ONE TO LAY EGGS NOW.

DON'T BE SO SURE. REMEMBER THE QUEEN CELLS?

Ms. Frizzle led the way to the queen cells. Two new queens emerged at the same time.

After they had dried out, they had a terrible fight. One queen stung the other queen to death!

Then she killed the other queen pupae in their cells. Now she was the new queen.

TWO QUEENS? I THOUGHT...

THERE WAS ONLY...

ONE QUEEN IN A HIVE.

A QUEEN BEE CAN STING MANY TIMES by Arnold
Unlike worker bees, which can sting only once, the queen bee can pull her stinger out of the victim and sting again.

YOU WERE ABSOLUTELY RIGHT.

THE STRONGER QUEEN SURVIVES TO PASS ON HER STRENGTH TO HER CHILDREN.

35

QUEENS MEET DRONES
by Wanda

Thousands of drones from many colonies gather in one place.

When queens are ready to mate, they fly there, too.

Usually drones do not mate with the queen from their own colony.

ANOTHER WORD FROM DOROTHY ANN

Nuptial comes from a word that means "wedding."

The worker bees pushed the new queen out of the hive. Ms. Frizzle said she was going on a nuptial flight — a flight to mate with drones.

AFTER THE NEW QUEEN MATES, SHE'LL RETURN TO THE HIVE AND START LAYING EGGS.

HER EGGS WILL HATCH AND REPLACE THE WORKERS THAT LEFT WITH THE OLD QUEEN.

THEN THE HIVE WILL BE AS STRONG AS IT WAS BEFORE.

MAYBE YES, MAYBE NO...

Drones

New Queen

36

After the new queen left,
we heard heavy footsteps.
It was a bear, trying to steal the honey
and the bee larvae!
The workers flew out and tried to sting the bear,
but its thick fur protected its body.

MEANWHILE

BEEKEEPER STILL ON THE WAY

IF THE BEAR BREAKS OPEN THE HIVE...

AND EATS ALL THE HONEY AND THE LARVAE...

THE BEES MAY NOT SURVIVE!

WE HAVE TO HELP!

STING HIM!

I CAN'T GET THROUGH!

HELP!

COMMON HIVE RAIDERS
by Tim

Skunks ➜

Bears ➜

Wasps ➜

Bees from other hives ➜

Bees can defeat most robbers, but bears are hard to beat.

BEWARE

NEVER GET CLOSE TO BEARS. THEY MAY LOOK CUTE, BUT THEY ARE VERY DANGEROUS.

We flew out and dived at the bear, but it kept coming at the hive. "We have to use strategy, class," called the Friz. "We'll lure the bear away!"

BEE FOR ANYTHING PREPARE

BE A BEE! DEFEND THE HIVE!

BUT I DON'T WANT TO HURT A CUTE LITTLE BEAR.

I WOULDN'T SAY CUTE AND LITTLE.

I'D SAY BIG AND HUNGRY!

Ms. Frizzle made a beeline for the beehive-bus —
and we followed.
The jar of honey that had spilled before was
still on the floor.
The bear smelled the honey and came after us.
"Ms. Frizzle!" we yelled. "Do something!"
She stepped on the gas, and the bus lurched forward.

THE BEAR WILL FOLLOW OUR HONEY AWAY FROM THE HIVE, CLASS.

MS. FRIZZLE SPILLED THAT HONEY BEFORE WE CHANGED INTO BEES...

AND BEFORE WE BECAME BEAR BAIT.

THOSE WERE THE GOOD OLD DAYS.

UN-BEARABLE

As we rounded a corner,
the honey jar rolled out the bus door.
As the jar fell, it returned to its normal size.
The bear started eating honey and forgot all about us.

Ms. Frizzle reached for a joystick
on the dashboard.
To our relief, the bus lifted off.
It wasn't a beehive-bus anymore. It was a bee-bus!
Down below, we saw the new queen returning home
from her nuptial flight.

THE HIVE IS SAFE!

WE'RE SAFE!

WE'LL MEET THE BEEKEEPER
ANOTHER DAY, CLASS. RIGHT
NOW, WE'RE RETURNING TO
THE CLASSROOM.

IT'S ABOUT TIME.

41

We returned home from our flight, too.
The instant its six feet touched the ground
in the school parking lot, the bee-bus changed.

It was a full-size school bus again.
We were human kids again.

BUSY BEE RIDDLES

Q: Why do bees itch?
A: They have hives.

Q: Why did the bee hum at her singing lesson?
A: She didn't know the words.

Q: How does a bee fix her hair?
A: She uses a honey comb.

Q: What grade did the students get on their honey project?
A: They all got B's!

REPORT CARD

And back in the classroom, we thought of the perfect project to end the day: baking honey buns, of course!

I KIND OF MISS BEING A BEE.

YES, I FEEL LOST WITHOUT MY ANTENNAE.

I LIKED THE STRIPES.

THE BEST PART WAS THE HONEY... AND WE CAN STILL GET THAT FROM BEEKEEPERS!

BYE-BYE BEES

Magic School Oven

To: Ms. Frizzle and her class

BOB'S BETTER BEES

HONEY FROM BOB'S BEEHIVE

HONEY FROM BOB'S BEEHIVE

44

45